Playing Church

Quitting the Game, Being the Church

Danna Batten

Author's website:
www.dannabatten.com

dannabatten.com

Playing Church/Quitting the Game, Being the Church by Danna Batten Published by Danna Batten Platte City, MO 64079 www.dannabatten.com

Cover by Brittany Jobkar.

ISBN-13: 978-1724539038

ISBN-10: 1724539035

Acknowledgements

I am eternally grateful for the never-ending love and support of my husband, Mike Batten. He makes all my adventures possible. Also for my son, Daniel, who has given me a greater understanding of our heavenly Father's heart toward us. I'm also grateful for my faithful friend, Eilene Senter; the watchful and helpful eye of Vicki Lipira; my amazingly creative friend, Brittany Jobkar; and awesome photographer, Missy Moore; as well as all my friends and family who have walked through life's journey with me.

Introduction

Are you tired of playing the games those around us insist we play? I believe we are in a time when many Christ-followers are struggling to live in the freedom that Jesus' death has bought us. Danna Batten has written a book that can truly help you navigate the "games" in church life. As she says in the first chapter, "…life is full of games. They are in relationships, work, family dynamics, politics, and even the church." So how do we find a way to live life the way Jesus intended us to live? How do we avoid the games in which so many of us are trapped? This book provides many of those answers.

I first met Danna in 2014. I truly believe God brought her to our church at just the right time. You see, at the time, I had been in full-time vocational ministry for around thirty-five years, and I was beginning to realize that there were people in the Church as a whole who were looking for answers about how to live life differently than they had always lived. They were looking for a way out of their brokenness and wanted to find freedom from the victimization of past traumas, abuses and injustices.

I have spent so many hours during my ministry counseling people who have found themselves in broken places, unsure of how to live in freedom and joy. Christ-followers do not escape the circumstances that can weigh us down. But fortunately, we have the truth of Christ to help us navigate the storms of life. Jesus came to give us life to the full. Danna states, "…Jesus, with His last breath, said, '*It is finished*,' meaning everything has been accomplished. The healing you need from the trauma you've experienced is available. Jesus can heal any emotional, physical, or spiritual wound you have…[we] must participate with Him to receive it."

When Danna and her husband, Mike, began attending our church, I was in a season of life when I was seeing a Christian counselor. I was in the process of finding freedom and healing and knew that so many other people needed to experience that as well. I discovered early on that Danna had the gifts to help others navigate life in a healthy manner. She is an expert in this area and has helped many people find their way after having faced many struggles herself. She is an active part of our leadership team, and I regularly ask her to preach, teach classes and counsel in ministry at Tiffany Fellowship Church, where I am lead pastor. Her ministry has changed the lives of many, and I love that this book extends that information to everyone.

Just as in the game "Simon Says," Simon will dictate what we do, so we begin to let the voices around us dictate what we do. Those voices tell us how to play the games of life correctly, or so we think. Even the lie of negative self-talk becomes a loud voice. Jesus, the voice of Truth, needs to become the loudest voice in our lives.

This book is filled with stories from Danna's life that will speak to everyone, of every age. It will help you find answers to life's games. So what are you waiting for? Turn the page and discover how to escape the scourge of *"Playing Church."*

REVEREND BARRY N. CLAIR, LEAD PASTOR

Tiffany Fellowship Church

Kansas City, MO

Table of Contents

Chapter One

Playing Church

I could see the frustration building on my face as I stared at my reflection in the bathroom mirror that Sunday morning. My heart swelled and I cried out, "There has to be more, God! I don't have time for playing church!"

As I stood there, pondering the sweetness of the previous evening my husband, Mike, and I had shared with friends, I wondered, how did I get to this place of "playing church"? We had had an amazing time, sharing with friends about what God was doing in our families and church. We prayed for one another, lifted up prayers, dreams and desires God had put inside each of us. It was precious and real! The kind of moments Mike and I seek out with those with whom we do life.

But playing "games" is a waste of time, and I decided that I no longer want to be a part of it. I was done trying to live up to the expectations and requirements of others—or even my own self-inflicted demands—in order to be a "good" Christian.

As I turn fifty, it seems the years keep getting shorter and shorter, and the hours move faster with every day. Time has become a precious and valued commodity. Having fun, experiencing life and celebrating events (both difficult and good) together are not what I'm looking to change; these are the things authentic living is about. But I am finished with rules and regulations that cause me to feel as if I need to earn something in order to "be enough," "make the grade," to be accepted or used by God.

When I got saved, my new life seemed pure and sweet. I had an overwhelming understanding that God loved me so much that He gave His Only Son that I might be His. But what has eventually clouded and distorted the ease of this relationship? This question took me back to childhood memories and where I first learned how to be a participant in the "game."

I remember my kindergarten year of school. There was a kitchen station, along with dolls and cribs at the back of our classroom. This is where I learned the art of "playing games." When playing house, we each established clear roles and defined how they should be played. Everyone played their role happily until someone stepped out of line or attempted to perform another aspect of the game, as if they had forgotten their place in the house. Acceptance in the house was based on one's willingness to play "fair" and within the boundaries set by whoever was in charge that day. I learned quickly where I fitted in and what was expected of me in order to play house, because, when I didn't follow the rules, whoever was boss quickly yelled, "Mrs. Schmidt!" Mrs. Schmidt would come over and ask what was wrong and remind me to "play nice." I knew that meant I was to do what was expected.

This was my beginning training: life is full of games. They are in relationships, work, family dynamics, politics, and even the church. Now don't be getting all mad and defensive. I love the Church, my own church, and the brothers and sisters in Christ that I know and have met there over the years. They are the very reason that I've come so far from where I was, a lost and lonely woman who still felt like an unwanted little girl. What I'm referring to are the expectations and requirements set up by us humans to keep us following the rules and playing nice. This is what I no longer have time for.

I'm pretty much a black-and-white, right-or-wrong, kind of person. Sure, I've always tested the limits of those confines, but in the end, I know what I should do, and normally do it. This is why playing games had always felt so comfortable for me. Once I knew and learned the role, understood the expectations, and located the boundaries, I could play my part. This is exactly why it was so hard for me to understand that I had gotten caught up in the "game" and what was happening to me after all those years of trying so hard to perform well.

Why did I feel dead and lifeless inside a body that on the outside I could make look as if I had it all together? What was I doing wrong? I thought I knew how to play the game. I didn't realize at that time God was removing me from the game so that I could experience real relationship with Him and others, without the restrictions of expectations. Out of a place of "doing" church and into a place of "being" the Church where we don't have religious obligations but a love affair with Jesus.

This may sound harsh to some, and honestly, it once did to me as well. But really, now I just want to follow with abandon whatever God wants me to do, not what man expects of me. And I don't have the energy to pretend I'm something that I'm not. This is freedom: Living a life of grace, knowing full well that I'm not perfect—and God doesn't expect me to be—and that others aren't, either. Acknowledging that it's not my job to fix them but to love them. Trusting God to take each of us to the whole and complete person He has designed us to be. Being individuals who live and love with a passion for the lost, becoming like Jesus who came to seek and save those who do not know Him.

Because I had learned how to play the games so well, it took me a long time to come to this place and recognize who I really am and still be able to love and accept myself as well. Often there is a chasm between what we know and what our hearts believe, a space that looks so small, but without much experience is in fact, vast. Oh, that you might *experience* the love of God (though it is so great we will never fully understand it) so you can be full of abundant life (see Ephesians 3). The Lord wants us to wait upon Him, look for Him; and if we keep knocking, we will find Him. Recently the Lord spoke these words to me.

> The fullness of love, fullness of joy and fullness of peace is waiting. Just beyond the door of this world into My presence where you may be transfixed by the beauty of My glory. The place where discovery never ends, all you need will be found there. Come away and see the many facets of who I am: great and mighty, strong and sure, the same until the end. Hear Me as I sing over you; dance in the freedom of My love. This world will grow strangely dim as you are washed away in My love. The depths of it will take your breath away. I am your Father, come away with Me and you will see things greater than you can even think or imagine. Taste and see that I am good. I'm waiting. Come away!

Having the freedom to move around outside of what was expected felt like unfamiliar ground. However, this new place without walls has allowed me to breathe. Taking in air without limitations has brought such joy into my life. Fear has begun to fall off as I stretch out to the possibilities of God and learn to walk in step and obedience with Him.

I'm so glad He allowed me to see what was happening, because, if He hadn't, I would still be "playing church," believing it was the right thing to do.

"Are you tired? Worn out? Burned out on religion? Come to me. Get away with me and you'll recover your life. I'll show you how to take a real rest. Walk with me and work with me—watch how I do it. Learn the unforced rhythms of grace. I won't lay anything heavy or ill-fitting on you. Keep company with me and you'll learn to live freely and lightly." (Matthew 11:28–30 MSG)

Chapter 2

Hula Hooping

It was hot, and my emotional temperature was rising along with it. I'd been practicing all afternoon. For the fourth time, the Hula Hoop around my waist crashed to the ground.

In the early 60's, the Hula Hoop™ made a big return to the market when the toy company, Wham-O™, reintroduced it. Twenty-five million hoops were sold in only the first four months and over one million in two years. Hula hoop contests became all the rage, even in my backyard. This brought with it a twirling of these amazing rings around our waist, legs, arms, ankles and neck. The hoops, like an array of color spinning quickly around, caught us up in the fascination and fun. I loved my hula hoop and played with my friends, often seeing who could keep theirs up the longest or who could whirl the most at one time. One of the girls was a year older than me and could keep her hula hoop whirling longer than the rest of us. I watched with envy and frustration as she demonstrated her skill and ability to spin more than us all; she was continually developing the art of the game. As hard as I tried to be like our backyard-world-record-holder (my idol), no amount of practice could make my waist and arm turn consecutively. We quietly discussed strategies among the less adept on how we were going to attempt our win in the next competition. This game, like all the others we played, became about impressing my friends, proving I could keep the most "hoops" dancing midair.

As I grew, without my even intending it, my life became about this same game. "Keeping up with the Joneses," some call it. Even though keeping up with the Joneses may have been the initial intention, being the best was really the goal.

You know what I mean, don't pretend you don't. There have been moments in all of our lives when we strived to be better than others, to be the proclaimed winner over others, the envy of all. It happens at work, with friends, and for many of us, even in our churches. My sisters and I had this competition going on between us to prove who was best. My older sister was naturally smart and popular. From my perspective, she "had it together," and I wanted to be better than she was. I wanted to be able to do more things, have more friends, and get more attention than her. We fought like cats and dogs while growing up, trying to prove we each were the best. I'm so thankful that with maturity our relationships have changed into ones in which we love and stand with each other; my family is precious and faithful. We now love and appreciate our differences and who we are. It was never God's intention that we all be exactly the same.

At a very young age, I remember the pressure I felt to perform well, to be the best in catechism class. Doing all the work and memorizing what was required got you a star. You were known to everyone as having it all together. This rating system continued as I grew. Good behavior and perfect attendance in grade school got you a star as well. This resulted in candy at the end of the quarter. In middle school, whoever dressed the best and had the most friends became the most popular, which was the star on the chart for this season. High school brought other criteria into the mix of the game. Not only were dress and friends required, now one needed to be in the most activities, drive the nicest car, and get good grades. All while making time for having the greatest boyfriend. Boy, the game got harder, as it required me to spin more and more hula hoops than ever!

Now, I want you to know I believe in honoring those who do well. However, often these competitions unintentionally teach us that it's about performing well and outdoing others, not setting and achieving goals. Whoever could keep up the most "hula hoops" without losing it determined who was best. That is exactly what happened in my heart as I grew. I wanted to be the best, get the appreciation, and show others I could keep up more hula hoops than they. I worked hard to be accepted and approved of by others, to find out their expectations and determine to meet them. Seeing the look of approval on someone's face meant my performance was accepted. I was learning to play the game well.

Then I entered my twenties, which brought with it marriage, work, and being the best person everyone could count on. I could do everything, have everything, and if I didn't, I wasn't measuring up. At this point in my life, I was not going to church, because who had time for it? Besides, I had blown it so many times already that I thought they probably didn't want me playing there, anyway. I bought into the whole I-am-woman-hear-me-roar game and was working really hard to balance all the plates (keep up the most hoops) required, because I *had* to have it all together.

In my formative years, the 1960s and 70s, women were being influenced by Betty Friedan's book, *The Feminine Mystique*. Women everywhere were stirred to anger because they felt Betty captured their frustration, even the despair of a generation of housewives who were trapped and unfulfilled. I, along with many others of my generation, bought into the feminist movement, to the point of believing I was unimportant unless I did, and had, it all. Not only was it required to *do* it all, but to do it the best.

At the time, I was a wife working full time. We built a house, had nice things, and entertained a lot. I always looked put-together, never went without makeup, and got the praise of those around me. My house, my yard, my clothes, my husband and my life were always perfectly managed and groomed. At work I got promotions and won the approval of those who were important. However, to my disappointment, with all this praise and acceptance, I still felt empty inside. Wasn't I playing the game right?

This confusion only caused me to strive harder, stuff my feelings of inadequacy, and perform more. Often, I laid awake at night planning and scheming how to keep it all together. Self-help and motivational books weren't helping either, no matter how many I read. I couldn't possibly let anyone know how exhausted I was or how fear of what others thought of me was my constant prod to do more. The thought of someone thinking I couldn't handle it all was terrifying. Everyone else was doing it, what would they think?

One day it all came crashing down; I could take the pressure no longer. All the "hoops" I had been spinning for so many years, dropped. It was four years into our marriage when the pressure of trying hard and still feeling unworthy crushed me under its weight. Turning toward my natural instinct of running when things got too tough, I left my husband and ran from anyone who cared about me. The unbearable pressure I felt left me unable to process my thoughts clearly; I was drowning in a sea of confusion. Nothing anyone attempted to say made it better, it only added to my need to silence everything. I completely refused to talk to friends and family and moved into a small studio apartment, alone and separated from everything that required anything from me. I was unable to communicate with friends and family because I couldn't even answer the questions that were racing within my own mind. Exhaustion from pretending and performing for so long had overtaken me. I had known all along I wasn't perfect but was determined that no one else would know it.

> For we have all become like one who is unclean, and all our righteousness (our best deeds of making us right) is like filthy rags or a pollute garment; we all fade like a leaf, and our iniquities, like the wind, take us away far from God's favor, hurrying us toward destruction. (Isaiah 64:6 AMPC)

Miraculously (as He has done so many times in my life), God intervened. I found my way back home, and from there, back to the church. I was broken, beaten and bruised from what life had thrown at me and the choices I had made. My attempts to hide those broken places and still win the game had left me but a shell of a person. With much counseling, prayer and drawing near to God, I began to experience healing from my striving. My strength slowly began to return as I built relationships with God and others in the church.

However, that familiar game of "hula hoops" found me again, this time in the church. Because it was familiar, I picked it up fast. I learned the expectations and requirements it took to rise on the Good Christian Chart, and I began getting "stars." I took all the classes, attended seminars and training.

Whatever hoop I was expected to jump through in order to arrive at my goal of being a "good" Christian, I played the game with gusto. In some classes, I was told if I prayed more this would happen, and then others said if I knew the Word better I would arrive. Service was also a key: Good Christians must serve in the church, show they were involved. I got busier and busier, to the point I didn't even have time for my own quiet time some days. Then I felt like a failure because I wasn't doing what I was supposed to. I was spinning as fast and as hard as I could, not realizing all along that it was for nothing. To God, my attempts to please Him were as filthy rags.

Sure, people were noticing what a "good servant" I was, which opened more doors of opportunity for me. I got to a place that almost, if not every, evening I had something to do or someone to care for. My family was falling second to my, or someone else's, perceived needs of others. I was working hard to prove myself to God and others. Even with all these attempts I continued to feel empty and worn out. Again, I found myself confused, because I thought I was doing what I was supposed to do. This was the example I saw in church.

In Bill Thrall's book, *Truefaced*, he calls this the "Room of Good Intentions." He describes this as a place of striving, of trying to please God, and calls it the room of "Striving to Be All That God Wants Me to Be." The very name of the room indicates that we may believe our value comes from a motive of trying to please God and then our actions follow in that same vein. We think our value comes from being "all God wants me to be." Bill says the fact is that it isn't our efforts that please God but learning to live from a place of trusting that we are who He says we are. Loved and valued, not because of what we do, but because of Whose we are.

My frustration and anger continued, which began to build division in my marriage relationship, until one day my wise husband said, "That's enough." With his help I began to see the needs I was not meeting at home and the necessity to set wise perimeters for ministry. This outline consists of seeking God first in all things and doing what He wants me to do, not what others expect from me, along with the understanding that recognizing the first ministry I am called to is to my family.

> Trust in the LORD with all your heart; do not depend
> on your own understanding. Seek his will in all you
> do, and he will show you which path to take.
> (Proverbs 3:5–6 NLT)

Balance began to return in my life as I understood I was not responsible for everyone and everything. My obedience to God was where my focus should have been set. He hadn't put a requirement of performing on me; in fact, He died to set me free. So, why was I attempting to please others? The game. Which was is not God's plan for me or anyone else in the church.

In Galatians 3, Paul asked the question, "How foolish can you be? After starting your Christian lives in the Spirit, why are you now trying to become perfect by your own human effort?" (Galatians 3:3 NLT) This is why I was tired and empty in my own attempts. Instead of listening to and following the leading of the Holy Spirit, I got caught up in pleasing others. It was my faith (trust) that pleased God all along, not my perfection. Not in keeping up the hula hoops.

These days my fear of what others think rarely rears its ugly head. I find that saying no gets easier with age and as I grow in the confidence of His love for me. There is a sense of security that comes when you know you're chosen and adopted into God's family and that there is nothing you need to do or can do to earn it. Learning to listen to and follow the Holy Spirit's leading was my only way out. I needed to stop following all the other voices I had been following, as is done in the game of Simon Says.

Chapter Three

Simon Says

"Touch your nose." My hand almost rose to my nose before I realized that "Simon" had not said it. "Simon says touch your nose." Fingers on my and all my friends' little hands rose up to be placed on our noses. Giggling erupted as we nervously waited which command would come next.

You remember the old familiar game of only doing what Simon told us to do. If we did something Simon had not instructed us to do, we were "out," having to sit on the sidelines as others dutifully followed Simon's demands.

Thinking back on this game, I'm reminded of all the voices I've followed over the years, and the destruction that came with many of them. These voices could have come from within me or from others. I'm not talking about requests or instructions from an appropriate authority figure in my life; I'm speaking of the voices I was never intended to follow. There are voices that lie to us about ourselves, others, and even God. But we follow them, believing we are doing what is expected.

Sometimes those voices come from people we are trying to please or whose approval we are attempting to get.

Other times they are simply the enemy's attempt to cause us to believe lies, lies that will separate us from others and from God so that we can be more easily "taken out."

> Stay alert! Watch out for your great enemy, the devil.
> He prowls around like a roaring lion, looking for
> someone to devour. (1 Peter 5:8 NLT)

Our enemy, the devil, does not want us walking in truth. He wants us deceived so that we will not be able to recognize the voice of the Holy Spirit, which leads us into all truth. This is why he will use others or even our own thoughts to speak lies to us or about us. Most of us have had both experiences and have suffered from their consequences one way or another. My life has been no exception to this. I too have believed lies and listened to the wrong voices, which have led me down some wrong paths.

Some of those voices are the voices of others that have devalued me and caused me to be unable to see who God created me to be. They have said things such as, "You will never be good enough"; "You always mess things up"; and, "You're such a disappointment." Words, voices and lies that told me I was worthless and undeserving of love. I lived believing this about myself until I was nearly thirty years old. No wonder I lived my life trying to get the approval and acceptance of others. Then, even if I did get that approval, I still didn't believe it or trust it, because my belief system had been founded on the lies.

Other times, it happened through someone not intending to mislead me, but who was in a position of influence in my life, and they themselves didn't know or follow the truth. This could have been a teacher, a boss, a parent or even a church leader. One such event happened when I was in the fifth grade.

It had been a really hard year for me. I was sent to a new school and didn't know anyone. Not only was everyone unfamiliar to me, I was at that awkward stage of puberty. "Uncomfortable" was my middle name. It's the season in life when everything is changing and you don't know what to do because all you've ever known was the freedom of simply being a kid. I didn't like myself, school, or life. I wished there was a rock I could crawl under until it all passed.

I struggled most with one particular class: Science. It was never my favorite, and now to add to the mix there was a teacher who was harsh. One day as he passed out worksheets, he informed us we were to work silently at our desks and to come up to his desk only if we had questions. Today I don't remember the specific subject, but what I do know is that it was a concept that I just could not figure out. To my embarrassment, I had already been to his desk two times and still needed help. Swallowing my pride and the lump in my throat, I stood to walk across the room once again. Before I got half way to my destination, he stated loudly for the whole class to hear, "Don't even bother me again, you obviously won't ever get it." A blanket of shame dropped over my shoulders as I hurried back to my desk. *Where was that rock?* How could I hide from the staring eyes of the other kids in the class? The enemy's arrow of destruction penetrated deep into my heart that day as I began to believe I was a disappointment and a failure, who would never be smart enough.

The enemy has compounded lies in my life through church authority figures, as well as others in positions of authority. Because of their words, fear ruled over me; all of which caused me to doubt and to not trust God. At times, I was taught and shown that God was harsh and demanding. That He was watching out for me to do wrong and that payment was required for the wrong. However, the truth is that Jesus paid it all. He ransomed me because He loved me.

Also, I was taught by other voices that sin has different levels of severity. This instruction was demonstrated to me through both word and deed. People looked at those who gossiped differently than someone who had had an affair; or say, a little white lie was not as bad as getting drunk. However, as I began to listen to the voice of truth through the Word of God, I discovered these things were not true, all sin has the same result: it brings death and destruction. The fact is our consequence of sin does have different results and degrees of severity. Not only was some of the instruction I received incorrect; at times, there were spoken negative implications about myself or others. It saddens me to this day that because of such wounds many have left the church. And I am forever grateful that by God's grace I am not one. My hope that truth will be the center of every church service and Christian organization is held not on account of man but on the fact that Jesus said, "…and upon this rock I will build My church, and all the powers of hell will not conquer it." (Matthew 16:18 NLT) Fellow believers, no matter what has been spoken to you or about you by someone in the church, the enemy would love to destroy your relationships. Turn to Jesus who is the author and perfecter of your faith. God will accomplish what He says He will in His Church!

Often the loudest voice that lied to me was my own. Because of experiences I had had and things that had been spoken, my inner thoughts bombarded me continuously with lies. *You're worthless, unusable, too broken, unwanted, ugly, imperfect, a failure, undeserving.* You know the thoughts, we all have them. I pretended I was something else, but deep inside this is who I believed I was. One such instance happened as I walked into a woman's conference where I was speaking. Inside me a voice said, "Who do you think you are? You're a mess. No one can learn anything from you." We can be our own worst enemy; often what we speak to ourselves is not truth. It is imperative for our spiritual health that as disciples we follow God's instruction to take our thoughts captive.

> For the weapons of our warfare are not carnal but mighty in God for pulling down strongholds, casting down arguments and every high thing that exalts itself against the knowledge of God, bringing every thought into captivity to the obedience of Christ. (2 Corinthians 10:4–5 NKJV)

This is exactly why we must protect and guard our minds with the truth of God's Word and follow not "Simon" but the Holy Spirit's voice.

What is truth? Jesus is. He said of Himself, "I am the way, the truth and the life." (John 14:6b NLT) Where can we find this truth? In the Word of God. John the Disciple tells us: "So the Word became human and made his home among us. He was full of unfailing love and faithfulness. And we have seen his glory, the glory of the Father's one and Only Son." (John 1:14 NLT) Jesus is, was and will always be truth. It is through His life and the Word that we can know, walk and trust in truth. Truth is not found in anything of this world, only in the One who created it. We need to stop listening to Simon's voice—all the voices of this world—and learn to follow Jesus.

This is possible for all of us; Jesus would not have said it if it wasn't true.

> "My sheep hear My voice, and I know them, and they follow Me." (John 10:27 NKJV)

Now if you're like I was, you're asking, "How can I hear the voice of someone who is not here?" and "How am I supposed to follow Jesus?"

We can hear and follow Him through His Word—the Bible—and the Holy Spirit. Scripture tells us that the Word is alive and active. As we read it, God speaks to us through the power of the Holy Spirit that lives inside every believer. This happened to me one day while reading First John: "See how very much our Father loves us, for he calls us his children, and that is what we are! But the people who belong to this world don't recognize that we are God's children because they don't know him." (1 John 3:1 NLT) The words jumped right off the page for me, and for the first time I knew that God loved me and wanted me. I realized that all the other voices I had been listening to were not true. I was worthy of love, and God wanted me.

Jesus gives us very clear instructions about the Holy Spirit in the Gospel of John, chapters 14, 15 and 16. The Holy Spirit is our way to have a relationship with Jesus, though He may not be living on this earth any longer.

> "He is the Holy Spirit, who leads into all truth. The world cannot receive him, because it isn't looking for him and doesn't recognize him. But you know him, because he lives with you now and later will be in you." (John 14:17 NLT)

Our lives are to be abundant, not through ourselves, but through the power of the Holy Spirit, which is the promise that Jesus spoke about in the Gospel of John. We will start there and see what Jesus said about the Holy Spirit and what He would help us do. Before we do, I think it is important that we understand the framework of what was happening when Jesus was speaking this to the disciples. It was Passover when He was sharing a last, intimate dinner with those whom He loved. He knew it was the final time He would be sharing with them before His death.

I don't know if you have experienced these last moments with someone you are close to, but I have. My dad passed away eight years ago. I remember those moments like they were yesterday. He knew that only days remained for him to be on this earth, few precious moments before we would see him no more. He spent that time reassuring us and sharing with us the most important things he wanted us to remember.

He was in the hospital and we intended to bring him home on hospice that afternoon. My sisters and mom ventured to the cafeteria to grab a bite to eat before we left the hospital. I sat quietly watching TV with my dad in his room. He gently touched my hand and said, "I want to die, but I don't know how." His statement shook me to my core as I realized I didn't have an answer; do any of us really know how to die? All we've ever done is learn how to live. Tears trailed down my cheeks as I swallowed hard so I could respond. "I know, Dad, it's okay." Silence veiled the room as we cried softly together.

Only moments later (though it seemed a lifetime), my mom and sisters returned and saw the scene unfolding. I shared with them our conversation and said we needed to pray that the Holy Spirit would come and show him how to go

Home. Right after we finished praying, my dad had a vivid moment of clarity through the haze of pain medications and spoke a very personal and specific encouragement to each of us. The intimacy of this point in time will forever be etched on my heart and in my mind.

This is exactly where we find Jesus and the disciples, in an intimate moment He did not want them to forget. What do we see Him talking about? The Holy Spirit. This is exactly why it is so important that we, as disciples, understand, know about and walk in a relationship with the Holy Spirit. It was that important to Jesus. In John 14:15–29 and 16:7–15, John describes to us some of the things that the Spirit will do. He

- will always be with us (will never leave you),
- leads us into all truth,
- will be in us,
- teaches us everything and reminds us of what Jesus said,
- reveals our sin and our need for Christ (conviction),
- tells us about the future (this is prophecy),
- tells us whatever Jesus says.

Jesus was speaking intimately with His disciples with these words, because He did not want them to be afraid or confused when He was no longer with them. He also knew it was best that He leave, because then the Holy Spirit could come and fulfill all that He was to do in His relationship with them. However, He knew the disciples would not want Him to leave. These were words of assurance and encouragement that, though they would not see Him physically, He would never abandon them. He wanted them to know who the Holy Spirit was and how the Spirit would relate to them in His place.

Just as we can recognize the voice of someone with whom we have an intimate relationship, we are able to recognize the Holy Spirit's voice. It takes the same to build a relationship with the Holy Spirit as it does with a good friend or spouse: the investment of time, along with sharing and listening to one another, as we develop awareness and are attuned to one another.

There are primarily four ways we can hear from the Holy Spirit: Through the Word of God, His voice, wise counsel, and our peace.

The Word is one that we've already addressed. It speaks as we read it or meditate (think) on it. And because the Holy Spirit lives within us, we can hear His voice. Jesus describes this to His disciples by saying, "the Spirit of the Father who speaks in you." (Matthew 10:20 NKJV) Like being able to recognize the voice of a friend without seeing their face, we too can learn to identify the Holy Spirit's voice. This voice will always line up with God's Word. If it doesn't, it really is "Simon," so do not listen to it.

Wise counsel can be another way that the Holy Spirit may speak to us. Proverbs instructs us to seek out the advice of others so that God can establish His plan and direction through it. The counsel it is speaking of as wise is from one who has their own personal relationship with God. Otherwise, what they may be speaking from is not truth.

Then last, peace may be a way that God speaks to us. Paul told the Philippians that they were not to be anxious or worried, because if they told God what they needed, God would assure them by giving them peace. When our hearts and minds have peace, we can know that we are walking where He wants us to walk. If we are not at peace within ourselves, we need to ask God what is causing the unrest.

I will hear what God the LORD will speak, For He will speak peace To His people and to His saints. (Psalm 85:5 NKJV)

To me His voice is the sweetest sound I know. I continually ask that the Holy Spirit attune my ears to it in a greater measure. In my life, it is the thing that can bring peace in a storm and wisdom to a situation.

During a counseling appointment with a woman who showed up at our church one day (no one knew her because she didn't attend there), God spoke to me about her circumstance and brought breakthrough. She and I had been talking for about an hour before this happened, and I was beginning to think that I was not going to be able to help her. Quietly, to myself, I prayed, "Lord, I've got nothing. I am asking for wisdom." In that very instant God revealed to me through a vision an event that had happened between this woman and her father in their kitchen.

Would I listen to God's voice or blow it off as my imagination? As in the game of my childhood, would I do what Simon said? My experience of His faithfulness allowed me to trust Him and step out in what He had shown me. I said to her, "Do you remember the time in the kitchen with your dad when…", and shared the entire vision I had had. As I spoke, tears welled up in her eyes and began to trickle down her cheeks. By the time I was finished, her head was in her lap and she was sobbing. Once she regained some composure, she asked how I knew about that. I told her I didn't, but God did, and He wanted her to know He saw it all and He had never left her. God began to open her eyes up to the truth regarding her dad and their relationship. He brought healing, forgiveness and freedom to her that day by what He spoke.

I am so thankful that, as I have developed a relationship with Jesus, I have had the privilege of hearing from Him in these ways. Now, because I love Him, I want to do whatever He asks. I willingly follow where He wants me to go. I don't do it perfectly, but God knows it is my heart's desire.

Chapter Four

Dress Up

"What will I be today? A princess, a bride, or a ballerina?" The possibilities before me were endless. It really didn't matter which I chose, because I knew with certainty that as soon as soon as I slipped on a particular sparkly gown, I would become the most beautiful girl in the world.

Most girls, if they're like me, remember the days of seeing their mom's makeup, pretty dresses and high-heeled shoes and wishing they were old enough to wear them. Or maybe most boys were like the boys I knew, wanting to be the greatest superhero, cowboy or athlete. We all had dreams of what we wanted to become and imagined we were something other than who we really were. That's why as little kids we learned how to play "dress up."

It was an amazing moment when I was able to open my mom's makeup drawer and try on some eye shadow or lipstick. Or slip my feet into a too-big, high-heeled pump. I looked like someone with war paint and unable to walk, but what I saw in the mirror was beautiful. On rare occasions I might find a crown or sparkly jewels and become a princess who had everything she wanted, including a prince.

In the neighborhood I grew up in, there were mostly boys, so I played dress up inside. But when we were outside, I played along with them. We took towels or blankets, tied them around our necks making capes, and became amazing superstars of the universe. Riding our bikes to protect and defend the helpless! Or, sometimes we carried toy guns and ropes and became cops and robbers or cowboys out on the range as we rode the streets around us. What fun we had!

Behind all the coverup, I pretended I was someone else, usually a famous movie star or model. It wasn't me I was dreaming to be. I wanted everyone to believe I was someone more important, beautiful, famous or talented than I could ever be. The older I got I continued (without realizing it) to play the game of dress up. I became what others wanted me to be. I did what it took to fit in.

Though this game started as fun dreams and imaginations as a child, it became a lifestyle as I got older. I remember it started for me in middle school, some of the most awkward times for most of us. I didn't feel comfortable in my own skin: what I looked like or how I thought others viewed me. So, I would discover what the most popular people were like and try to become like them. Most of us have experienced this feeling in one way or another. Our natural fix-it, to cover what we deem inadequate. This continued into my high school years as well, but with increased importance.

It was during these years that not only did I doubt my acceptance, I also made choices that brought me shame. This shame fueled my need to cover up what I did not want others to see. As time passed, I began to understand that this art of "dress up" got me the influence and things I wanted. It got me into the group of friends I wanted, as well as other relationships. Even jobs and other opportunities eventually opened up to me. I loved that through this game of pretend many doors were opening up to me, even if at the time I didn't recognize the cost of it all.

I perfected the art of this game, though I was mostly unware of doing so. I even started to forget who I really was and began believing the lies. That's what happens. We begin wearing masks in hopes others won't see our flaws. We lose ourselves behind the masks. Believing it is necessary because we want to project the perfectness all the "makeup" has to offer. We become pretenders caught up in the trap of Satan.

> "And watch as I take those who call themselves true believers but are nothing of the kind, pretenders whose true membership is in the club of Satan— watch as I strip off their pretensions and they're forced to acknowledge it's you that I've loved." (Revelation 3:9 MSG)

We are having identity crisises: the world, individuals and even some churches. Lies are distorting the truth in such a way that confusion is rampant, and people are falling prey every day to the enemy. Satan is robbing us of our inheritance. Traumatic events in our lives can also distort the reality of our prospective, and we are unable to see clearly because our "lenses" have become colored by these events.

When I was in high school, I was date raped. This traumatic event changed how I saw everything. In my eyes, myself, men, others and even God became so distorted by pain and disappointment that I didn't want anyone to know the real me. I told no one because I was so ashamed and embarrassed. I remembered the words I had heard spoken by others about women who had been raped. "Well, she shouldn't have gotten herself in that position. It was her fault she was there or it would not have happened." No, no one would know about my experience. I couldn't risk the exposure.

Silence was the first layer of makeup that became my mask of sadness. Sadness was then covered up with hopelessness, and eventually, I was overtaken by self-hatred. I no longer liked who I was. On the outside no one knew. My mask was so secure that I looked like I had it all together. I was dying inside, and not a soul could see. Fear became my constant companion. Fear of what others thought, fear of rejection and judgment, fear that I would never be known and loved for who I really was.

I continued to live in this trap through most of my young adult life. I even brought it with me to the church. I could tell that certain people were more accepted and the really put-together ones were allowed to serve in positions in the church. This became my aim, and fueled my drive to be needed and accepted by those I saw as "good" Christians. I did all the right things, said all the right things, and wore all the right things, until I began to be welcomed in these groups. Despite going about it in all the wrong ways, I really wanted to be pleasing to God. But, I found myself pleasing only man.

My fear of what people thought of me began to trump what God thought of me. Not only did I find myself in this place, but so many in the Church today live there too. I've talked with and ministered to people who are exhausted from trying to please man. They strive to be what others require of them in order to be accepted or to have the opportunity to serve in the church. All because they believe that if they don't, others will reject them.

Not only have they believed these things, but the harsh reality is, sometimes the Church has held people to these standards. This happens when leadership operates out of fear and its need to be in control. A little of both were my reasons for wearing masks and playing dress up in church. It was only as I developed my personal relationship with the Lord that the light of His truth began to expose how I was living.

> The Lord's light penetrates the human spirit,
> exposing every hidden motive. (Proverbs 20:27 NLT)

As I grew to know Him more, I realized that He knew me. Not only did He *know* me—every good and every bad thing about me—but He *wanted* me. Not because of who I pretended to be, but because I was His and He loved me. For someone who lived in a place of rejection and conditional love, this truth took time to penetrate my heart.

Despite the lie we may be living in, our subconscious never forgets what lurks behind the mask. It remembers that lying right beneath the surface is all that we are trying to hide. This was why it was hard for me to feel safe without covering up. I had done it all my life and really didn't know how else to live, or what image to project.

> So God created human beings in his own image. In
> the image of God he created them; male and female
> he created them. (Genesis 1:27 NLT)

I discovered it was God's plan all along that I was created to be like *Him*, not like others. All of my attempts to be and feel wanted had been a waste, because God already accepted me and designed me perfectly. I didn't need a mask or to play dress up to receive His approval. It was through the power of His Holy Spirit that I could be transformed into who He created me to be. For this to happen I had to let all my own attempts die and forget all that this world had taught me about what I needed to be. The apostle Paul puts it this way: "Don't copy the behavior and customs of this world, but let God transform you into a new person by changing the way you think. Then you will learn to know God's will for you, which is good and pleasing and perfect." (Romans 12:2 NLT) My thoughts and belief systems about myself, God and others needed to be reset. So, where and how can we fix the identity crisises in our lives? Only our Creator, Father God, can tell us who we are and restore our identity.

> He came to his own people, and even they rejected him. But to all who believed him and accepted him, he gave the right to become children of God. They are reborn—not with a physical birth resulting from human passion or plan, but a birth that comes from God. (John 1:11–13 NLT)

All the lies and all the trauma from our past can be made new through the power of the Holy Spirit. Our identity can be restored, and we can step into the fullness of our inheritance. However, it will require us to participate with Him in destroying the enemy's assignment against us. Ephesians 4:22–24 tells us to throw off the old sinful nature and our former way of life, which is corrupted by lust and deception. Instead, let the Spirit renew your thoughts and attitudes. Put on your new nature, created to be like God, truly righteous and holy.

Do you see what our part is? "Throw off" and "put on." Second Corinthians 10:3–5 tells us to do this: "We are human, but we don't wage war as humans do. We use God's mighty weapons, not worldly weapons, to knock down the strongholds of human reasoning and to destroy false arguments. We destroy every proud obstacle that keeps people from knowing

God. We capture their rebellious thoughts and teach them to obey Christ." (NLT)

When you or I recognize we are walking under a lie, we must take it captive, which means to stop thinking it. Then we replace it with the truth, which is God's Word. And, we keep doing this every time the thought returns, asking God to change our thoughts. As we do, God will restore to us the truth of who we are.

Now let's consider how we are healed from trauma. Jeremiah made this confession of where our healing comes from.

> "Heal me, O LORD, and I shall be healed; Save me,
> and I shall be saved, For You are my praise."
> (Jeremiah 17:14 NKJV)

God is your healer. He sent His Son to purchase your healing and freedom with His blood on the cross; by His stripes you are healed. And Jesus, with His last breath, said, "*It is finished*," meaning everything has been accomplished. The healing you need from the trauma you've experienced is available. Jesus can heal any emotional, physical, or spiritual wound you have. Again, however, you must participate with Him to receive it.

First, we need to ask for healing. I remember thinking, *How many times will I need to ask?* The answer is: as many as it takes. Keep knocking. Consider this: If a doctor told you to take some medicine to heal you, would you take it just once? No, you would take it as long as you needed to in order to be healed. It may take more than one request, but God is always faithful.

Just recently I had an area on my skin that was a concern, even to those in the medical field. I kept finding excuses and being busy, so I wasn't making the time to go get it checked. And, now as I look back at my thoughts and feelings, I can say that honestly I didn't want to know what it was. So, my husband and I began to pray for healing each morning, and then after church service one Sunday, I had our healing team leaders pray for me as well. After a couple weeks, the spot was almost completely gone, only a little speck the size of a pinhead remains. I am going to continue to pray, ask and seek for complete healing and restoration. How long? As long as it takes. I know that I can trust God to complete the good work He is doing in me.

Other times, because God is always about relationship, it may require reaching out and asking others to pray for you.

> Such a prayer offered in faith will heal the sick, and the Lord will make you well. And if you have committed any sins, you will be forgiven. Confess your sins to each other and pray for each other so that you may be healed. The earnest prayer of a righteous person has great power and produces wonderful results. (James 5:15–16 NKJV)

James tells us our healing comes when we have others pray for us; when they stand in agreement with us and with God for our healing. God is always about relationship and connection with Himself and others. This way, when we feel weak, we still can find strength through Him as others hold up our arms. Do you remember that victory came for the Israelites against the Amalekites because God promised to give it to them as long as Moses held up his arms? What happened when he got weak and tired? Aaron and Hur, his helpers, held his arms up for him. (See Exodus 17.) At times, it is no different for us when in the battle to get back the inheritance the enemy has stolen from us. As we fight this fight against our enemy to destroy the lies we have believed and heal our past, we step into the fullness of the inheritance God intended for us.

For me, this was a process that happened over several years. Even today, there are things the Holy Spirit reveals to me that are lies and I bring them to Him. With each lie that has been exposed, I have confessed it as sin and asked God to renew my mind in the truth of His Word. It's been a purposeful work of allowing God to rewire my thoughts. And, as I have, He has made me new, and I now believe I am loved.

A couple months ago, after finishing over sixty hours of personal ministry for the individuals that had come through my last healing course, I found myself being drug down by the lies of the enemy and began believing I was inadequate to help others. Thoughts began bombarding my mind: *Who do you think you are? You don't know what you're doing, you can't help anyone. What do you have to give?* The noise of the lies got so loud that the feeling of incompetency drove me to a place of wanting to run. Run because it was hard, and run because I didn't want anyone to know I didn't know what I was doing.

I realized I had gotten caught in a trap and was listening to the wrong voice: Only our enemy condemns us. Our heavenly Father never speaks to us that way. I began to cry out to God, asking Him to renew my mind in the truth and heal the past wounds that started this deception in my life. As well I contacted a close friend and asked her to be praying for me. That day, after praying, I stood on our deck, watching a hawk being chased and thrown off course by a flock of crows. I said the Lord, "This is what I feel like, all the noise is derailing me and sending me off the path You have put me on." It was embarrassing to admit after all these years in ministry that I was struggling.

On my walk the following day, as I was continuing to ask God for help, telling Him I wanted to not be afraid or to battle doubt, a movement on the horizon captured my attention. Flying across the brilliant blue sky was a hawk, rising above the clouds, soaring on a wind current. Behind him was a single crow, and despite making as much noise as the crow could, the hawk stay firmly on course. My breath caught in my throat as the Lord spoke these words to me: "You will not be overtaken, I am with you. You will rise up out of your doubt and soar on eagles' wings. Your past does not define you. I have given you everything you need to be all that I've called you to be." With tears flowing down my cheeks, I finished my walk, singing praises to God.

It has also required that I remove my mask and get real, open and honest with God, and sometimes others. Only by allowing myself to be vulnerable and allowing others to know who I really am and allowing them to walk with me through the process have I found true healing. This hasn't always been easy, but the freedom of living in the light, being fully known, has been amazing. At times, I can't fathom who I used to compare myself with to what now God has done in my life. It was for my freedom that He was willing to die. This is the unconditional love my heart desired all along.

As I stopped pretending and started being who I really am, to my astonishment, I found this was the very way my life could glorify God. He will use a broken vessel that doesn't cover or hide.

So all of us who have had that veil removed can see and reflect the glory of the Lord. And the Lord—who is the Spirit—makes us more and more like him as

we are changed into his glorious image. (2
Corinthians 3:18 NLT)

God's amazing grace has allowed me to minister, write,
preach and teach these truths to others. Not because I am
something special, but because He promised to turn all the
ugliness in our lives into something beautiful. If there is
anything I want to leave with you, it is a promise Isaiah spoke
of (see below). The hope for all of us who hide, pretend, and
attempt to cover what we don't want others to see.

"The Spirit of the Sovereign LORD is upon me, for the
LORD has anointed me to bring good news to the
poor. He has sent me to comfort the brokenhearted
and to proclaim that captives will be released and
prisoners will be freed. He has sent me to tell those
who mourn that the time of the LORD's favor has
come, and with it, the day of God's anger against
their enemies. To all who mourn in Israel, he will give
a crown of beauty for ashes, a joyous blessing
instead of mourning, festive praise instead of despair.
In their righteousness, they will be like great oaks
that the LORD has planted for his own glory." (Isaiah
61:1–3 NLT)

All along, God's plan for our lives was that by His death
on the cross we would all be set free from anything that holds
us captive, and to turn our sadness into joy. He died so that all
the pain, shame and difficulty in our lives could be made into
something beautiful so that others might see how awesome
our God really is. Let's take off our masks, dear ones!

Chapter Five

King of the Hill

"You're not on top, I am!" came the heated shout from my friend. "I pushed you off! I'm the best and you know it." I understood his irritation. I was positive that I had pushed Jeff off the hill yesterday, and now he refused to budge. It just wasn't fair. It was my turn to be "king."

As kids, we used to play King of the Hill. The object was to stay on top of the hill, or pile, designated as the "throne" (the high place), the longest. Other players attempted to knock the current king off the pile and take its place, thus becoming the new king. As I stated earlier, we lived in a neighborhood filled mostly with boys, so this was not always a successful game for me. But in my competitiveness, I strove to not let the boys beat me. However, I rarely had the strength to knock off the oldest of these boys, Robby. If the others and I teamed up, though, we found this could be a strategy to defeat him. Push him off the hill and become the next king, on the top at last!

We had fun together, though sometimes what got bruised most was our pride. That's what caused us to gather others to be on our side. You know, the whispers and the gestures to get someone to see things from your perspective.

And then, suddenly the object of our offense was on the outside of the group and needed to be knocked down. There were times the competition got us so up in arms we ended up as two groups of kids, not playing together for days. Pride does lead to the *fall*. Sometimes that fall included more than one person.

It wasn't until many years later—and being knocked off several hills in my life—that I recognized much of what I thought was competitiveness was actually my pride. Pride sneaks around, often undetected, in our lives, ministries and even our callings. Just like when we were kids, our pride wants us to be right, demands to be noticed, and will do what it takes to draw others to it.

As I type these words, it grieves me to see where in my own life I have lived, wanting to be King of the Hill. I wanted the attention, recognition and power that came from being on top. This desire has broken relationships and hurt others. It's a game that causes great destruction, not only in our own lives, but in the lives of those we have knocked down in order to get there.

I've realized that much of this is rooted in the fact that as a child I didn't feel accepted or valued for who I was. Even with my sisters, I competed for attention in an attempt to be recognized. When you grow up with this void, a desperate hunger drives you to prove your worthiness. You crave attention, and that creates a demand for others to fill it. As I grew, my enemy, Satan, continued to use different events and people to fuel my belief of being worthless.

I remember one day getting to a point that, even with all my attempts, the chasm kept getting bigger. I decided I was not going to care anymore. I put myself in the position of the permanent ruler. No one was going to tell me what to do, and no one would get close enough to hurt me again. I would do whatever I needed to in order to stay in control, and I'd use whatever power I had to manipulate people and situations to get my way. It was during this time that the ugliness of control hurt those around me. Eventually my kingdom came crumbling down around me, because I had pushed everyone away with my attempt to rule.

> "For rebellion is as the sin of witchcraft, And stubbornness is as iniquity and idolatry. Because you have rejected the word of the LORD, He also has rejected you from being king." (1 Samuel 15:23 NKJV)

My life began to look like something from the C. S. Lewis's book, *Mere Christianity*: I was full of pride. Lewis says that people experience pride when they have more than someone else, but this is different than just about having "things." Our comparison is what makes us proud, believing that we are better or above the rest. If you remove the element of comparison, then pride goes as well.

When you are the only one in your kingdom, there is no one else to rule. That is where my hardness had brought me— all alone. And when you're alone with your own unworthiness, there is no place where you can find your value. You can only find value from your Creator, because He formed you. He alone knows your purpose. Isn't it true that a table can't say to the carpenter, "I'm a chair"; neither can a vase say to the potter, "I'm a flower." They weren't designed to be a chair or a flower, their creator fashioned them for the desire he intended; both of which, when functioning as destined, brought glory to the one that formed them.

Pride is our demand to be right, our demand to be heard, and our demand to be in charge. This position leaves no room for anyone to speak into our lives and keeps everyone at a distance. The distortion is that our attempts to prove we are worthy are actually preventing us from relationships that will give us worth. God our Creator is waiting, longing and desiring for us to come to Him. He won't demand it. His commitment to giving us free will, the ability to choose Him, stops that. Pride, the original sin in the Garden by Adam and Eve, always separates us from God.

Adam and Eve existed in perfect harmony and communion with God, walking uninhibited and free from the need to demand their own way, because He had given them the Garden to watch over. However, Satan lied and convinced them that they could be like God. It was pride that opened the door for them to choose to disobey God; their right to do what they wanted to do. As we know, this discussion allowed the entrance of shame into their lives, and they hid from God. A hindrance from intimacy was set in place. Their demand to know all, be on top of the "mountain," only really separated them from relationship.

Often, we don't see pride in ourselves because pride is fault-finding. We forget that what irritates us about someone else is often because of its reflection in our own lives, so pride will look for another person to blame. Pride also causes us to look at others with contempt and judgment, instead of love and mercy. A prideful person is often defensive because, instead of standing in Christ's righteousness, they have to defend their own; so if challenged or rebuked, they will tend to fight back. Like the fallen angels of Heaven, pride will make us hungry for attention, causing us to demand respect and worship from others. Pride will also go after power, causing us to view others for what they can do and what they can give to us, rather than being aware of someone else's feelings or needs. In truth, we all struggle with pride in its hidden forms at some time or another. This is exactly why we are warned so urgently about it in Scripture. God knows it will lead to our fall and destruction.

Consider moments when you tried to be on top, what you did and what it took to get there. People you may have used, hurt or walked on in the climb. It never made you closer to anyone, unless they were clinging to your coat tail, trying to go with you, and that was never true friendship, anyway. You really just hope no one will ever find out what you did. Often we experience shame because of what we did, so we think covering up is a better solution than letting others know the truth. This prevents us from living authentically with others.

Brene Brown is a PHD researcher who has studied shame. When speaking at TED Talk, she defined shame as an "intensely painful feeling" when we believe we are "flawed." We feel "unworthy of love and belonging" and "unworthy of connection."

But, the truth is that vulnerability is the entrance to living an abundant life. In her book, *Daring Greatly*, Brene writes that with vulnerability we experience feelings of emotional exposure, risk and uncertainty. She says that vulnerability is really the beginning point of love, belonging, joy and courage.

Everything we really wanted—acceptance—is found in being real. Now, that is a lightbulb moment for some. God is always inviting us into relationship with Himself; He never stops wanting us. This was true for Adam and Eve as well. Just look at His response to them after they ate from the tree He had asked them not to.

Then the LORD God called to the man, "Where are you?" He replied, "I heard you walking in the garden, so I hid. I was afraid because I was naked." (Genesis 3:9–10 NLT)

Right in the middle of them doing the very thing He told them not to do He invites them back into relationship: "Where are you?" There is absolutely nothing that can separate us from His love. He wants us to walk in the confidence of not who we want to be, but of who He created us to be. There we will find purpose, belonging and the fullness of joy that an intimate relationship with Him can give. Being fully known and fully loved at the same time, gives us the courage to do whatever He asks us to do. What seems unsafe really ushers us into perfect peace. We no longer need to be on top, we just need to be beside Him.

As we walk beside Him, we deal a death blow to pride, submitting our will to His will. Remember my telling you about my dad saying he did not know how to die? For weeks after my dad's death, God revealed so much to me about this battle to live. As I have thought about his statement, I've decided it is true, we don't know how to die. All we have ever done, since we were babies, is strive to live. Attempting to gain and to have whatever we need in order to survive.

I'm not saying this is all bad, I just want us to consider that our (my) flesh fights against the very thought of death with every breath. Death both physically and to our own will. However, as we are disciples, death is supposed to be a normal part of our lives. In the Gospel of Mark we are told that death unites us with Christ. Jesus told a crowd of people they had to give up their own will and follow Him if they wanted eternal life. This truth means that we must learn to die so that we might really live.

Death is part of being a disciple of Christ. You are no longer "king" when you die. Yet, the death that is required of us is not physical death; it is our willingness to give up our rights, our will and our way, and, instead, making the choice to trust, obey and follow Jesus. Paul tells us in Galatians 2:20 that death is our way to identify with the cross and what Jesus accomplished through it. Through the cross we are no longer subject to the Law of Moses as the Israelites were. Before Christ's death, they were required to follow all of the Law perfectly, in order to remain in right relationship with God. An impossible task, as it would be for you and me today. After Christ's death, a believer "crucifies" himself—puts himself to death—by choosing to say yes to God. Anytime we deny our own will, we are sharing in Christ's sufferings.

If we are going to be honest with ourselves, this is not always easy, because we like being in charge. There are moments in my life, and I am sure in yours, in which everything within us wants to demand our own way. Our way, our timing, and whatever makes us most comfortable. The feeling of our flesh dying is not pleasant, so we often want to run from it; or sometimes we just don't know how to "die," just as my dad didn't.

In the sixth chapter of Romans, there is an emphasis on dying. First is dying to sin and living for righteousness, and second is putting to death our old man so that we can have new life, which requires us to let go of our wants. In this portion of scripture, Paul mentions the word *know* three times. It's a doctrine he wants us to understand. The common thread is that we are to identify with Jesus through His death, burial and resurrection. Formerly, under the Law, Jews had identified with Adam's sin and condemnation. Now, because of what Christ has done, when we trust that He is King, we no longer need to make ourselves right, we know He made that payment for us. Jesus not only died *for* our sins, but He died *unto* sin, and we died with Him. If we trust in the payment He made, you and I can the live in the promise of resurrection power. This is great news!

As we come off our mountains and give ourselves over to God, we die to our old way of living. That desire to follow our own wants and ways leaves as we allow Him to be Lord of our lives. This is the only way in which we will experience the freedom for which Christ's resurrection made the way: by walking, living, moving and breathing in God's strength and will. That will lead us to abundant life.

I have experienced these very junctures, needing to come down off the high hill I found myself on. I once experienced an incredibly painful betrayal of a close friend, one that was so surprising it seemed to take my breath away. One afternoon while mowing, I began stewing and complaining to myself, replaying the event over and over in my mind. Not a pretty picture I know, but that is what happens when we allow pride and offense into our lives. About an hour into my tirade, I heard God speak to me, "Are you done yet?" The words weren't mean or harsh, just an interruption to my thoughts, an attempt to see if I was ready to die to my own will. My response was, "Yes, but…," and I continued on with my complaining. Again, the gentle question came to me, "Are you done yet?" Finally, I fell silent as my pride stood directly in front of me and I could not deny it any longer.

I began to pray and tell God I didn't want to forgive, my hurt wanted to demand staying on top. Finally, by His amazing grace, God broke through and I was able to die to my will and chose to forgive my friend. Trusting that, as I did, God would also heal and change my heart.

Christ came, died, and rose again so that we might have resurrection life and power both here and in heaven. In and of ourselves we want to figure it out and make it work how we see best. The truth is that you and I were never meant to be king over our lives, or anyone else's.

Chapter Six

Not Picked

"Today we are going to play baseball," our PE teacher said, over the roar of all the kids in the class. "This can't be happening again," I whispered under my breath. Humiliation was certainly headed my way.

Maybe this has never been you, but most of us have experienced at some time or another being the last one picked for a team. Whether it was a childhood game, at work or even for ministry, the impact of this rejection can be devastating. Lies formed from such events can form wrong belief systems about ourselves and others.

I remember feeling fear rise up in my stomach as teams were being decided for PE class when I was in elementary school. I wasn't the best at sports, nor was I the worst, but what happened in those moments, to me was an indication of my value and acceptance. Baseball was the game of the day, and I was not very consistent at hitting the ball. I knew others had seen this demonstration at prior events, so I held my breath with my eyes fixed firmly on the ground as teams were chosen. To my relief I was not last, the girl who couldn't run fast was; though my second-to-last place gave me little consolation. In my heart, I knew everyone knew I was no good.

There have been different moments in my life when this same message was repeated. Competition in friendships, groups or clubs often left me feeling the same way. At times, even in my own family, I felt I wasn't measuring up to the standard. Conditional love and acceptance feeds this symptom in our lives. Striving and trying to earn a place can leave a person exhausted. Some even give up trying, because it doesn't work anyway.

When I was young I too thought of games this way; wouldn't it be easier to just not play, rather than risk the feeling of rejection?

But, the reality is, if we sit out completely, are we really living?

I remember one time a teacher saying that without risks, there is no reward. Life is full of risks. Some can be fun and invigorating; others are scary and terrifying. For me, the latter can be the struggle. I don't remember as a child being a big risk taker. I was never very brave that way. I liked playing it safe (remember: knowing my role). My experience told me that the moment I misstepped, I would be out of the good graces of the person I was trying to please. These wrong belief systems led me down many terrible paths trying to please others.

In high school, at times I did and said things that I knew were wrong, in order to fit in. Sometimes at work I laughed along with the crowd while they gossiped about another person. Fear that no one else would want me led me into a marriage that ended in divorce before I was twenty. Being desperate for love and acceptance and trying to fill that void of how we see best, leads to disappointment, shame and bad decisions. We attempt to gain a sense of safety and security from people and things in this world, not realizing that our satisfaction will not be found there.

My confession is that I seek what is comfortable, and if we are honest with each other, most of us do. When something is different and I'm not sure how it will look or feel, that can make me want to shrink back into my comfort zone where I know and can see what to expect. At times, I'm still tempted to live my life this same way. I want to know where, when and how things are going to happen.

If we lay our lives bare in the light of truth, not hiding anything, we will find this is the place most Christians live. Within our own limits, by our own ability to accomplish things, where we can determine what will happen next. Are the Christians of today the same as the Israelites of years gone by? Crying out for what is familiar, even when it isn't the plan that God has for them? Do we cry out for what will make us comfortable because it is what we once had? Beware: Those who seek comfort over the promised land of God will not step into the fullness He has prepared for His children.

This divide, caused by our fears, can seem impossible to cross, but the reality is that the chasm can be closed. Jesus bridged the gap. I love this:

> But now you belong to Christ Jesus. At one time you
> were far away from God. Now you have been
> brought close to Him. Christ did this for you when He
> gave His blood on the Cross. (Ephesians 2:13 NLT)

The cross was the bridge for the divide.

Today, the Church finds itself, just as we individually do, standing at the edge of a widening divide, which Paul warns us about in 2 Timothy 3. Look at the description he gives of what will be happening in the "end times."

> But mark this: There will be terrible times in the last days. People will be lovers of themselves, lovers of money, boastful, proud, abusive, disobedient to their parents, ungrateful, unholy, without love, unforgiving, slanderous, without self-control, brutal, not lovers of the good, treacherous, rash, conceited, lovers of pleasure rather than lovers of God—all having a form of godliness but denying its power. Have nothing to do with such people. They are the kind who worm their way into homes and gain control over gullible women, who are loaded down with sins and are swayed by all kinds of evil desires, always learning but never able to come to a knowledge of the truth. (Vss. 1–7 NKJV)

Paul gives us clear evidence of this widening space between what God intends for us (His people) and where we actually are, even describing how people will act in the last days: 1) with a form of godliness without any power, 2) always learning but never coming into truth.

He warns that the last days will be terrible times. Another version uses the words, *perilous times*. This warning (of perilous times) indicates that the culture and atmosphere will be very difficult and stressful. The same term is used only one other time in the New Testament, in Matthew 8, where it describes the savage nature of two men who were demon possessed. It is used in these two instances to indicate that things will become even more dangerous, and that evil will be strengthened as the end nears. Perilous times.

There are a couple of things that are of importance for us to understand as we read this letter from Paul to Timothy. First of all, Paul is in a Roman prison for the second time and without the hope he'd had in the past—that he would be leaving. Paul is aware the end of his life is near. The tone with which he writes seems to indicate he had reason for concern: Timothy was in danger of weakening spiritually. So, with a motivation of love—like a father—and a desire for the gospel to continue to be shared, it was penned. Today, we should hear these words about God's love for us and be encouraged to continue strong in our faith, completing the work of the gospel with the same listening ears.

The second is that when reading the narrative of what people will be like in the last days we see that Paul is not talking about people in the world, he is describing people in the Church. Shockingly (just as I'm sure it was to Timothy), Christians were looking just like everyone else in the world. I've taken some time over the past few weeks to wrestle with God over these issues in my own life, to take an honest look into the motives of my heart ("Search me, O God and know my heart, try me and know my anxious thoughts" Psalms 139:23), because it's so much easier to quickly say that none of that is me. Truth will set us free, and I want any gap between God and me, closed. Billy Graham has said, "Jesus has a great many that believe in Him; but few who are true disciples."

Just as Paul loved Timothy, God loves us enough to confront us with what will happen so that we can bridge the divide through our intimacy with Him. In order to understand how to build that bridge, we must become aware of why the divide happened. So, look at Paul's description of what the Church will look like in the last days.

- *Lovers of themselves.* Studies have concluded that we are now in the age of the most narcissistic culture ever. Twenty years ago, even fifteen years ago, if you had said that we would have worldwide interlinking systems where it was normal for people to share on a weekly, daily, or even hourly basis what they were doing, wouldn't we all have laughed? And yet, we find ourselves invested (some even addicted to) in relating in this manner. Always focusing on what is going on in our own little worlds and how many people are paying attention to us. Now, I use social media, so I'm not saying it's all bad, but it can become all-consuming.
- *Lovers of money.* A growing number of people are experiencing stress, and even suffering from depression, as our striving for more and more increases. America is the wealthiest country in the world, on average, with first-world problems, while the rest of the planet has third-world hardships. Now, I am not belittling the real struggles we sometimes have; losing a job or your income is really difficult. But the reality is that many times we turn toward finding security in our bank accounts, rather than in God.
- *Boastful and proud, conceited.* Instead of thinking of others first, our tendency can be to want all of our needs met, all the while gathering praise for our performances. Sometimes, this drives us to a place of unwillingness to be known for who we really are, so that we must perform and wear masks in order to be accepted. We boast about things, trying to get the praise of man.

- *Ungrateful.* More and more we see people living with an entitled mentality, not appreciating the good things that exist in their lives. This spirit is breeding great discontentment and even disillusionment in the body of Christ. When we fail to live grateful lives, our belief systems never have the capacity to believe God is a *good* Father.

- *Abusive, brutal, slanderous, without self-control.* Just watching the nightly news, we see that people are no longer living with restraint but giving full vent to their anger, feeling justified in it. Hatred and violence, in and outside the Church, is on the rise and widens the gap between God and His people. Words are being used to bring wounds and even destruction to those with whom we disagree. It grieves my heart that people are saying whatever they want, without even thinking of the consequences. The tongue has the power of life and death. Lord, put a guard on my mouth.

- *Lovers of pleasure.* Do you catch yourself (as I sometimes do) more often thinking about the next fun thing you get to do and the plans you're making, or are your thoughts on how your life can impact and help others? Enjoying life is not sin, but Christ gave us the example of laying down His life so that others might live. Compassion has become a thing of convenience, not sacrifice.

- *Unforgiving.* Holding onto grudges, not letting go of offenses, or "stuffing" painful events have left us bound in bitterness and resentment. We lack the willingness to, or sometimes the understanding of, our need to forgive. Yet, Scripture is clear that forgiveness is an act of obedience to God; however, we often hold on to what we believe is our right to the offense: "You just don't know what they did to me." This creates disconnect in our relationships, with God and with others.

- *Unholy.* Jesus instructs us to be holy, just as He is. If God asks us to do something, then He has made it within our grasp to be able to accomplish it. However, our holiness will never be produced through our own efforts; it may only happen through our connection to Him. Broken intimacy removes us from our source of power and our ability to be holy. You and I are set apart for *His* works and purposes, not our own.

I don't know about you, but I'm more comfortable saying, "Yes, the people in the world, this is who they are." But, *no*, Paul is saying this is who *we* are. The Church (and I, at times) has fallen prey to the enemy's schemes and bought into the lies of the world.

How can we be free from this snare of fear, close the gap of the great divide and build a bridge?

Look at the instructions Paul gave Timothy.

> But as for you, continue in what you have learned and have become convinced of, because you know those from whom you learned it, and how from infancy you have known the Holy Scriptures, which are able to make you wise for salvation through faith in Christ Jesus. All Scripture is God-breathed and is useful for teaching, rebuking, correcting and training in righteousness, so that the servant of God may be thoroughly equipped for every good work. (2 Timothy 3:14–17 NKJV)

Paul said, "But, as for you, Timothy...," and today he is saying, "But, as for you, Church...," be secure, strong and courageous. Hold on to what you have learned, not what you see. Don't get your eyes on the things of this world; keep your eyes firmly fixed on Jesus Christ, the author and perfecter of our faith.

As we do this, what will happen? We will bridge the gap.

First, we have been instructed to walk in the *power* of the Holy Spirit so that we may live godly lives and not live "having a form of godliness without power." Jesus clearly instructed the disciples to not "act religious" like the Pharisees but to lay hold of the power that the Father has promised. In the second chapter of Acts Jesus is speaking to those who believe in Him when He tells them not to leave Jerusalem but to wait, because the gift that His Father promised—and that He spoke about—would come to them there. When it did, they would receive power from the Holy Spirit.

The process of discipleship is the process of transferring the authority that we've been given as His children. A believer is someone who is on the way to Heaven, but a disciple is one who is bringing eternal life into the here and now: "Your Kingdom come, Your will be done, on earth as it is in heaven." (Matthew 6:10 NKJV) It's a transfer of authority. We have been given all authority through Christ Jesus, and it gives us the possession of power.

I heard a statement at a conference a couple months ago that just really shook me, but I really think it is what we are talking about here. Dr. Caroline Leaf said, "The church is full of atheistic Christians. They believe in God and are going to Heaven, but their lives have no power."

As a Christian psychologist, she continually sees an increase of Christians' powerlessness; unable to be free from sin, fear, depression and emotional dysfunction. Guys, Christ died to set us free, the power of sin was defeated at the cross when Jesus said, "It is finished." The Holy Spirit of God is living on the inside of us, the very same power that raised Jesus from the dead! Our lives are to be full of *power*.

But what are our lives producing? Scripture clearly says that Jesus' disciples will do even greater things than He did. Is this where we are living, is this where the Church is today? Do our lives look like a life of abundance? Full of love, full of joy and full of peace, spilling out onto those we encounter? We are to look different from the world because, you and I, we have a *good, good* Father.

Jesus tells His disciples (what you and I are to be) to go out and pray for people, so that the sick may be healed, those who are lepers can be cleansed, the dead can be raised up and demons cast out. We need to be praying for the sick, the brokenhearted and the captives, sharing with them the "Hope of Glory," with the confidence of being His child, trusting that wherever we are, there *He* is. We have everything we need!

He is wanting to use us as conduits through which Heaven can touch Earth. Do you, like Paul, truly want to know Christ and experience the same mighty power that raised Jesus from the dead? That means we must willingly step out (in the flow of power) into anything God would ask us to do, without fear, trusting that the grace is already there.

In his book, *Relentless*, author and Bible teacher John Bevere says we can go past our natural ability and strengths only with God's empowerment: grace.

Do we step out in grace? Are you willing to dare to believe and trust God?

Go and make other disciples, baptizing them in the name of the Father, Son and Holy Spirit, and teach them to follow truth. This is our assignment: evidence of *godliness* with *power!* Can you imagine a day when we (the Church) begin to look like His hands and feet, to the fullness that He has for us? People are healed when we pray, demons are cast out when we speak, and many are being changed and transformed by the gospel that our lives demonstrate. I want to go past my natural ability, into the "greater things." Our lives should be full of power!

Second, our learning must connect us with truth; in other words, what we are learning should change our lives. Paul instructed Timothy to "hold on to what you have learned and know to be true," because he knew our enemy would try to lead him astray. Deceiving words that sound good and feel comfortable are the spirit of this age, drawing many away from truth. We are, as Kingdom disciples, to hold to *truth* at all costs. Pastor Tony Evans describes "Kingdom Disciples" as someone who is not only a verbal but a visible follower of Christ who is continually learning to place everything under Jesus' lordship.

What is truth? It is Jesus. He said, "I am the way, the truth, and the life." Our lives and the perspective from which we live must align with what Jesus says, and who He is. Not what we see, not what we think, not what we feel, but with Jesus. Think about this with me: Are we truly living with absolute confidence of "who we are" and "Whose we are"? We have to be, if we are to be grounded in truth, connected to it.

Who are we?

We are created beings designed to be in relationship with our Creator. The moment you and I step into this exchange we become His children. This answers our next question.

Whose are we?

By adoption God calls us His very own. "God decided in advance to adopt us into his own family by bringing us to himself through Jesus Christ. This is what he wanted to do, and it gave him great pleasure." (Ephesians 1:5 NLT)

God wanted us, chose us, and adopted us into His family. There is nothing you or I can do or will ever do that would change His desire for us. Nothing can ever separate us from His amazing love.

Just for a moment, consider a parent's perspective. From the moment our son was born, when he became ours, something awakened in us to fiercely protect him. And, as our child, he recognized our voices, and trusted that we would take care of him.

The other day I got to meet my newest great niece (my eleventh). She is about two months old. Every time her mom spoke, her head turned in that direction, because, even at that little age, she knew with complete confidence who her mom was, and that she was hers. It didn't matter if someone else was holding her or talking to her, nothing disturbed her certainty of who she is and whose she is.

God wants us to know Him in this way: That we recognize His voice and we trust He is a good Father, wanting only the very best for each of us, His very own children.

Do you know Him in this way? What we are learning must connect us to this reality so that we willingly, completely submit our lives to His Lordship. What we're learning must connect us to truth.

Scripture is written for our instruction, so that we might know God, and from our intimacy, obey Him. We need to heed the words of Jesus so that we are not just saying the "right" thing but doing it as well.

> "What sorrow awaits you teachers of religious law and you Pharisees. Hypocrites! For you are like whitewashed tombs—beautiful on the outside but filled on the inside with dead people's bones and all sorts of impurity. Outwardly you look like righteous people, but inwardly your hearts are filled with hypocrisy and lawlessness." (Matthew 23:27–28 NLT)

We must allow the Holy Spirit to reveal to us the heart of the Father through His Word so that its transformative work can be done in us. This is how we are made into His likeness, as not just hearers but doers of the Word. We become a duplicate of the Master, so much like Him that we may be mistaken for Him. Aren't we to be His image to the world, showing His glory? So that as we walk around, what the world sees is not us but Christ in us.

When we know Jesus (Truth) intimately, we become free to be who He created us to be: His children, a coheir with Jesus, possessing the abundance of Heaven. Christ died, not only so that we may have eternal life, but also that we might live life to the full. God is calling all who want to stay safe in the boat with the same words He said in essence to Peter: "Come, come where I am calling you, do what I am asking of you. Walking though it may seem impossible. Step out of the boat where your surroundings may overtake you if I were not there with you. It is here that you will experience the fullness of life. Here where My grace is sufficient for you and My power perfected in you. When you walk by faith and not by sight, you are trusting in the One who knows the beginning, to the end. Though your eyes have not seen, I know, and hold the future in My hand."

So, from one who once believed that in comfort was where I wanted to be, I'm ready to step out in greater ways, into this adventure of following Jesus. Trusting Him with my life, my plans, the church, the world, my finances, my family, my lack of ability; knowing full well this is right where He wants me to be. We must get out of our pews, be willing to take risks and go into the world that so desperately needs Him. Though there may be wind and waves that surround me, He who is in me is greater than he who is in the world. Let's get out of our comfort zones and into His power. As a disciple of Christ, you have been "picked," chosen by God, to be the light of the world.

Chapter Seven

Hide and Seek

Anticipation rose up within me as I rounded the corner of house. *I know this is where she must be*, I thought to myself. *It is the only place I haven't looked.* Shocked to see only a vacant area surrounding me, I had no idea where to look now.

Ever since the time of Adam and Eve, we have played hide and seek. In chapter five, "King of the Hill," we discussed how they hid because of their disobedience to God.

As kids we played endless hours of hide and seek during the day, and even at night with flashlights. Out in the country night air, nighttime hide and seek was my favorite game. Sitting in complete darkness, watching the intermittent flash of a firefly, I peered out from behind my hiding place, only on occasion when I heard a rustling or voices nearby. Out from the black abyss, the only evidence that I was not alone came from the brightness brought on from a shining light, and I heard someone cry out, "You're it!" Now it was my turn.

Our goal was to be the last one found, because the first one found had to be the new seeker. The winner, the last one found, was the best at hiding. I can see where this characteristic—skill of the game—has carried over into my adult life at times. In my mistakes, I attempt to hide, because I don't want anyone to see my failures.

I once saw the cutest video of little children attempting to describe what love is. As you can imagine, their descriptions were adorable but also all over the place. They said things such as "sharing," "smiling," "saying nice things," "not being mean" and "hugging your mom." Love is one of those things that is often hard to understand, even for an adult, so how we show it to others can lead to confusion. Dr. Gary Chapman, a Christian psychologist, calls how we give and receive love, "love languages." Back in 1995 he wrote a book called *Five Love Languages*. In his book, Chapman tells us that one of humanity's primary emotional needs is love, and that for someone to be emotionally stable this need must be met. He explains that love gives someone the sense he or she belongs and is wanted.

In one of the chapters, "Love Makes a Difference," Chapman writes that there is one primary emotional need that we all have: Love. According to Chapman, studies by psychologists say love, as well as security, self-worth, and significance, is essential to humans. Love interacts with each and every one of these other needs. When we experience a sense of safety and are able to relax, we feel loved. Our value and worth grow when we feel loved, which is the very force behind much of what we do and who we become.

Not only does Gary Chapman explain our need for and the benefits of love, he also compiled a list of the five ways we receive love:

- words of affirmation
- quality time
- receiving gifts

- acts of service
- physical touch

Mike and I have led several marriage groups over the years. After Dr. Chapman's book came out, we used the book to help couples understand their love languages and how to communicate/demonstrate that love to each other. It was a powerful changing point in many relationships, because they understood how to show their spouse love in the way they could receive it. For some it was a lightbulb moment. For the first time they understood why their attempts at loving each other had not met those needs. All because they were loving their spouses in the way *they* received love, not how their spouses received it. I bring all this up because what caused such great changes in their relationships was the understanding that we all desire love to be demonstrated to us in different ways.

I believe that often in our relationship with God we can have this same confusion. Isn't it true, as I mentioned earlier, that even the word *love* is confusing because it is so misused and overused? Just think about it. How many times have you heard things such as: "I love that dress (or that car)"; "I love hiking (or some other activity)"; "I love cheesecake"; "I fell in love"?

Because of this misunderstanding of what love even is, and our often inability to demonstrate that love to others, we fall in and out of love, missing the mark. We are not loving others—and sometimes not even God—with his or her love language. This can cause us to feel as if we are hitting our heads on a wall, wondering, *What do I need to do?* Or even to the point of giving up in our frustration. Gary explained how we can learn to love others in a way that they will receive it.

So, what is God's love language? This is made perfectly clear to us in Scripture. Jesus told us how we demonstrate our love to Him. He said, "If you love Me, obey My commandments." (John 14:15 NLT)

And, in Deuteronomy, when God instructed Moses to give the Israelites His commands, He said, "Be careful to *obey* all these commands I am giving you. Show love to the Lord your God by walking in his ways and holding tightly to him." (Deuteronomy 11:22 NLT)

Do you see it? God's love language is obedience. We demonstrate our love by walking in His ways and obeying His commands. This is how we show our love for Him.

Let that sink in for a moment; let the lightbulb turn on. This may be a perspective change for some of us because many of us come from a "performance" mentality. This mentality causes us to try and work really hard at being "good enough." We think things such as: *If I just read my Bible more, pray longer, or serve more often, God will know I love Him.* A performance mentality, trying to prove our love to God. This has led too many people into a place of being worn out and burned out. Statistics tell us this is why many people leave the church, or even turn their backs on God; all this striving makes them believe they can never measure up.

All of this work, instead of simply obeying, which is what God has asked us to do.

Years ago, an amazing woman of God say to me, "Danna, just do the next right thing you know to do." I had been working really hard, trying to figure out how I could make sure God knew I loved Him. When, really, all I needed to do was stay in close enough relationship with Him, trusting that He would tell me what He wanted me to do.

Think of it this way: Have you ever watched the interaction of a parent with a child? The parent will make every effort to tell or show their children what they need to do. They are not standing back in some corner sneering, wondering if they will figure it out on their own. The parent is right there with them, guiding them along. God is no different with us. If He has said, "If you love Me, you'll obey Me," this means two things: First of all, He is speaking to us. Second, we have the ability to know what He is saying.

The questions for us are: Are you close enough to hear, and are you listening for His voice?

I believe this is why my pastor's, Barry Clair with Tiffany Fellowship Church in Kansas City, teaching on meditation was so impactful for me. It is one way of drawing near to God, training our ears to recognize His voice.

Also, I appreciate what Oswald Chambers says regarding prayer and meditation in his book, *My Utmost for His Highest*. He says that it is not about simply getting answers from God. It is about intimacy, about becoming one with Him. This is the place where we become complete.

He says meditation and prayer = connection. Most of us, as I have, thought prayer is to be spent telling God what's going on, letting Him know the answers we need, and sometimes even what those answers should be, instead of getting so close with Him. We are driven by the demands of our desire to perform. To be seen as worthy, productive, culturally relevant and "good Christians." All of which leads us to a place of striving instead of connecting. Our flesh fights against intimacy with God in every way, because the enemy knows we become dangerous when we still and quiet ourselves enough to get to know God. He knows that when this happens we learn to recognize God's voice, and then we are able to follow and obey Him.

A little over ten years ago, I was given a book, *Invitation to Solitude and Silence (Experiencing God's Presence)* by *Ruth Haley Barton.* Some of the concepts I learned from it were some of the most formative and transformative things I've experienced, because it taught me how to have deep intimacy with God, and I learned to hear His voice. This is where we all need to be, so close that we know even His thoughts and desires. In my life, learning to know what God wants me to do (and when I've been willing to obey) has allowed amazing things to happen. One such time was at a healing retreat that I was leading, and I could see a participant really struggling with something. During a worship session, she was lying face down on the floor. As I began to pray for her, God said, "Go over, sit next to her and rub her back." My initial thought was that is crazy. But, I was learning I could trust Him, so I did it. When I thought what my actions were supposed to accomplish was done, I got up and didn't see her until later that evening.

She came up to me and said, "Thank you. Do you know what you did?" I told her I just did what God had asked me to do. She began to describe what happened during that moment. She was battling with forgiving her mom over past hurts and was actually telling God that she couldn't do it. When I came over and started rubbing her back, God reminded her of all the times her mom had come in her room at night and rubbed her back while talking with her. In that instant her resistance broke and she forgave her mom. Revelation from God always brings with it breakthrough.

One day, unbeknownst to me, a friend was combatting frustration in her relationship with God, as she felt like her life was becoming twenty-yard dashes after Him, and then she'd quit because it wasn't sustainable. One day when she and I were together, God told me to tell her she would be running hard after Him in this next season. Recently I received a text that said, "I'm in a long-term marathon, determined to stay the course and pacing myself so it becomes my lifestyle, not just something I do." Obedience to God's voice brings hope to the hopeless.

Learning to listen to and obey God has not always been easy for me. It's not even always been comfortable, but when I did, my life never felt more full and complete. I've experienced great joy!

Think about a deep relationship you may have with a spouse or a friend, or even a relative. You have spent so much time with them you don't need to ask them what they would like you to do, you already know because you're so connected to them. Or, they can speak, and without you seeing their face, you recognize their voice.

Do we know Him that well?

Jesus did, and His life demonstrates this so clearly for us. Even at a young age He knew what His Father desired Him to do. In Luke 2 the story unfolds with Jesus as a twelve-year-old boy. He had gone with His family to Jerusalem for the Passover Feast. When it was time to leave, His parents assumed He was following along with the rest of the family to return home. But, after their arrival home, they discovered He was not there. They frantically rushed back looking for Him and found Him in the temple listening to and talking with the teachers. When they found Him they were amazed, and said:

> "Son, why have You done this to us? Look, Your
> father and I have sought You anxiously." And He said
> to them, "Why did you seek Me? Did you not know

that I must be about My Father's business?" (Luke 2:48–49 NKJV)

Jesus knew what the Father wanted and was in such intimate relationship with Him that He was doing what the Father wanted. This continued even as He grew older. In another instance He said this:

> "I do nothing on my own but say only what the Father taught me. And the one who sent me is with me—he has not deserted me. For I always do what pleases him." (John 8:28–29)

Jesus was always doing what His Father wanted Him to do. Because I see Jesus living this way is why obeying God is so important to me, as I am certain it is for you as well. I want God to know I love Him. Now, I'm fully aware I won't do this without mistakes, but I am confident He knows the desires of my heart. This I can rest in, not in my perfection, but in His love.

This word *obey* means that when we hear something, we should do it. We can't just know it and then not be moved to action. This is not love. In fact, Jesus explains this later in the Gospel of John. He says not obeying Him demonstrates our lack of love for Him.

> "Anyone who doesn't love me will not obey me. And remember, my words are
> not my own. What I am telling you is from the Father who sent me." (John 14:24 NLT)

Because we love God as Jesus did, we are moved to do what He wants us to do! We obey Him.

How can we have that intimacy Jesus had with the Father? How do we develop the connection of friendship so closely that we know the heartbeat of our Father? Jesus describes this close connection to be like the vines and branches of a grapevine, so close that our lives show evidence of this by producing "fruit," things that bring God glory. Then He continues by saying:

> "You are My friends if you do whatever I command you. No longer do I call you servants, for a servant does not know what his master is doing; but I have called you friends, for all things that I heard from My Father I have made known to you." (John 15:14–15 NKJV)

A friend is someone you feel safe with. They know everything about you and you know everything about them. It comforts you to know they are there for you and you can count on them. Friendship with God is just like this. He knows and wants what is best for us. This confidence should propel us to risk trusting God (taking steps forward), walking by faith and not by sight into the things He is asking us to do.

In Scripture we find someone called "a friend of God": Abraham. Abraham lived his life this way. God asked him to do something, and he obeyed. God asked him to leave all that he was familiar with and go to a new land. Abraham obeyed. Again, God tested their friendship by asking Abraham to sacrifice his son, Isaac. Because Abraham loved God, he moved into action to obey Him, trusting that God would provide a different sacrifice. Abraham loved God and that love continually propelled him to obey God. Abraham obeyed God because he loved Him, and God saw Abraham's love because it resulted in action.

As I said, I long for and desire such deep intimacy with God that I, just like Jesus or Abraham, will do or say whatever my Father wants. But, sometimes I place a wedge between us, and it stops me from following Him. I begin to believe the lie that it's not safe following and that I should be making my own decisions, doing whatever I want to do. These interruptions in our relationship are from either fear or pride.

In my moments of pride, I become unteachable. Stubbornness causes me to stop listening, because I think I know what's best. A superior spirit takes over and demands its own way. Pride causes me to want to be in control. The world feeds and fuels pride in us with all of its advertising and promoting of self. It tells us we should do whatever feels good and makes us happy. First John warns us about this interruption.

> Do not love this world nor the things it offers you, for when you love the world, you do not have the love of the Father in you. For the world offers only a physical pleasure, a craving for everything we see, and pride in our achievements and possessions. These are not from the Father, but are from this world. (1 John 2:15–16 NLT)

The other thing that can break our connection and our willingness to obey is fear. I believe fear is the enemy's biggest tactic against God's people right now. Fear is promoted through the media (everything we see is always bad). It is promoted through disasters that happen and through our changing world. Our own insecurities can activate fear in our lives.

This battle wages within our minds, and fear causes us to freeze and become unable to do what God is asking us to do. Scripture tells us we battle not with flesh and blood, but with powers and principalities. When we allow fear to drive our thoughts (which will dictate our actions), we are literally stepping into agreement with that principality and giving it power in our lives. A thought comes into your head: *Oh my gosh, what if (whatever it is) happens?* Then, instead of stopping that thought, we go down a path of: then this will happen, then that will happen; on and on it goes until we are in a spiraled frenzy of fear. In doing this, it causes the fear to get bigger than our God. So in our minds, whatever the situation, it becomes impossible and too big for God to do anything about. Second Corinthians 10:5 clearly instructs us to take our thoughts captive. We need to stop them immediately and not let the enemy lead us down these paths.

I don't know how often this happens to you, but it is a battle I have to fight to get my heart to agree with what my head knows. My fear leads me to stop trusting God and I am unable obey Him. This fear operates and is empowered in our lives when we lack an understanding of God's love for us. When this happens, we are unable to obey and submit ourselves under His care and let Him have control. This is exactly why we need to be intimately acquainted with God. As this happens, we know His love, and fear loses its power.

Not long ago, God and I had a conversation about an area of anxiety in my life. Anxiety is my nice way of saying I was afraid and not trusting Him. My twenty-year-old son has a motorcycle, and almost every time he is riding it, Satan loves to torment me with thoughts that try and make me forget how big God is. If you are a parent, I'm sure you can imagine what can run through my mind at night when he is out with friends. After a particularly late night, I went down the path of not taking my thoughts captive. By the early hours of the morning I could not sleep and was pacing the floor. To my husband's dismay, I kept waking him up. Please recognize my first mistake was allowing Satan to have power over my thoughts, which is what set me up for the course that lead me to the sin of unbelief. Second, instead of praying and stepping into intimacy and connection with God, I began to act on my fear.

Later that morning, when it was an appropriate time to be out of bed, God reminded me that He loved my son, Daniel, more than I ever could, so much so that He knew how many hairs were on his head and the number of days that he would live. He told me there was no amount of worry that could change the plans He had for Daniel, and that they were good, with an amazing future.

When we listen to our enemy's voice, we will always hear a lie. Our Father's voice reaches out to find us when we get off course and empowers us to obey.

Last, I want to point out what I mentioned earlier. Obedience means there is action, some sort of movement on our part. Whether that is physically or emotionally, we step into agreement with God. All we need to do to confirm this is look at the commission Jesus gave His disciples.

> "Therefore, go and make disciples of all the nations, baptizing them in the name of the Father and the Son and the Holy Spirit. Teach these new disciples to obey all the commands I have given you. And be sure of this: I am with you always, even to the end of the age." (Matthew 28:19–20 NLT)

Jesus said, "Therefore, go!" We are to go, move, do and follow what God is asking us to do. As disciples, we obey God because we love God. We *go* because we have true friendship and intimacy with God. We *go* because we are unafraid, trusting God has got us. We *go* humbly because He knows the plans He has for us. We *go* into the marketplace, the work place, our neighborhoods and our homes, bringing with us the Kingdom and the love of God. When we love God with His love language, we can change the world around us with His love because we obey Him!

Chapter Eight

You're Out!

As I peered out the window, I realized that over the past several months, once again I'd been experiencing a strange sense of longing I could explain only as a desire for more. Some sort of a deep understanding of which I'd only begun to scratch the surface: the faithfulness of our great God. I sipped from the steaming cup of coffee in my hand and let the vastness of everything I still didn't comprehend settle in.

It has only increased as I've been meeting with a good friend from Ghana and praying once a week. We've been crying out for the Church, God's radiant bride, asking that we be prepared for His return and that the world see His glory shining brightly from it. Together we've talked about the dynamics we've seen in the Church and how it demonstrates itself in the different places we've been.

One night I lay awake, unable to sleep, as a statement I heard recently stirred within me: "True passion demands action!" (Craig Groeschel with Life Church in Edmond, Oklahoma). The impact these words had on my heart forever changed me. Even now I struggle to explain what I believe these words contain for me and for the Church. Like a knife cutting through darkness they force me to look full on into my own experiences and what I've believed church to be, and all the confusion playing church has brought into my life. The truth that lies before me is that much of what church has been to me has been consumer driven: about meeting and satisfying my needs. I've looked for churches, programs, Bible studies, and events that will teach and train me to be a better disciple, searching for the things that will help my family to grow. Eating up (consuming) more and more teaching and instruction, becoming obsessed with learning more; yet, a lack of any evidence of it propelling me to movement.

God is warning us, His Church, not to become "barn-soured" Christians. When He spoke this to me, it immediately took me back to when I was young and to my years of having horses. If you have not been around horses, this may be an unfamiliar term; it is a horse that does not want to or refuses to leave the barn. It seeks only the comfort of food and the herd, and often wants only to eat and not leave the security of the barn. This is devastating to the production of a farmer who uses the horse in his operation, and can be just as bad for the animal. For me as a rider, it meant that Midnight, our Shetland pony, was difficult to train and sometimes even to ride.

I was on a trail ride one afternoon when I was nine. As our group of riders mounted the last hill, the barn came into view. Without warning, Midnight took off like a bolt of lightning across the field toward the barn. I held on to the horn of the saddle with all my might, because nothing I did or tried deterred him from his return to where he felt safe. As I bounced to and fro, my feet slipped from the stirrups and even our guide was unable to grab my reins in order to help me stop.

The anxiety a barn-soured animal experiences when it is required to leave the safety of its comfort zone can cause it to buck and rear, indicating its resistance to change. God used the picture of this event to encourage me to not stay only within the walls of the church, consuming the "food" provided and the solace of numbers. All that I have eaten/taken in should motivate me to share it with others.

The statement, "true passion demands action," requires me to ask: Do I have passion—the love of God—for others and the world around me? Is the Church showing the love of God to the world by its actions? How do we put love into motion? Are we—am I—willing to make the sacrifice that action will demand?

Honestly, I've done church in such a comfortable way that I'm not sure what change will look like or how to take those steps. But, I know deep within myself that I must. I am, as well as the Church is, to be a shining light for all to see the glory of God. It will require me to come out from under the "bushel" of my own comfort, being uncovered and exposed in my own uncertainty.

> "You are the light of the world. A city that is set on a hill cannot be hidden. Nor do they light a lamp and put it under a basket, but on a lampstand, and it gives light to all who are in the house. Let your light so shine before men, that they may see your good works and glorify your Father in heaven." (Matthew 5:14–16 NKJV)

When I look at the life of Jesus, I see One who walked this path. It was often a difficult and lonely way, because many did not understand. This is why my flesh cries out to remain under the basket where I feel safe and in control. I know what to do there, I know what to expect and what is expected of me. It's neat and clean, a place that I can manage with my own strength and my own capabilities. Jesus did things outside the box and it made messes. He stepped outside the religious norm into the power of God. Often, He would inconvenience Himself and His plans to have compassion on someone in need. After John the Baptist was beheaded, Jesus was on His way to find solace and be alone. Then He saw a huge crowd of people coming to Him for help and healing. Immediately, filled with compassion, He forgot His own need and changed His direction, taking time not only to minister to them but to feed them as well.

People wanted to kill Jesus for changing the look of their cultural activities. However, Jesus did not care, because He knew He needed to do what the Father wanted Him to do.

> "Therefore the Jews sought all the more to kill Him, because He not only broke the Sabbath, but also said that God was His Father, making Himself equal with God. Then Jesus answered and said to them, "Most assuredly, I say to you, the Son can do nothing of Himself, but what He sees the Father do; for whatever He does, the Son also does in like manner. For the Father loves the Son, and shows Him all things that He Himself does; and He will show Him greater works than these, that you may marvel."
> (John 5:18–20 NKJV)

Now that is someone who has come out from under cover and is standing high above the crowd with no fear of what others think, because He is confident in His relationship with the Father. Jesus willingly laid His life down in sacrifice and obedience to whatever the Father asked, no matter the cost. Even when His popularity plummeted and He was hated by others, Jesus stood fully exposed in the light of His Father's will. This willingness eventually led to His death and the fulfillment of all God had planned. Is my passion this deep?

The portrait of His life compels me to search my own. Have I experienced the Father's love to the measure I will walk wherever He asks? Ephesians tells me that this confidence will supply anything and everything I need. From the deep reserves of God's love, I will have the power to do all that He requests. This source is so great that even my imagination can't fathom all He has for me.

> I pray that from his glorious, unlimited resources he will empower you with inner strength through his Spirit. Then Christ will make his home in your hearts as you trust in him. Your roots will grow down into God's love and keep you strong. And, may you have the power to understand, as all God's people should, how wide, how long, how high, and how deep his love is. May you experience the love of Christ, though it is too great to understand fully. Then you will be made complete with all the fullness of life and power that comes from God. Now all glory to God, who is able, through his mighty power at work within us, to accomplish infinitely more than we might ask or think. (Ephesians 3:16–20 NLT)

I can't give what I haven't received. And, honestly, my own resources of love are far lacking to supply this need. Paul prayed for all of us to experience this love so that we might be made complete. It stands to reason there is a way for us to step into the abundant supply Jesus has. The experience Paul refers to is not a knowledge we perceive within our minds but learn from our interaction with or coming to know Jesus. Paul was fully aware it was this knowing of Christ Jesus that would allow him to become like Jesus. But, if Paul wanted to share in Christ's likeness, it would also summon him to share in Christ's suffering.

> Yes, everything else is worthless when compared with the infinite value of knowing Christ Jesus my Lord. For his sake I have discarded everything else, counting it all as garbage, so that I could gain Christ and become one with him. I no longer count on my own righteousness through obeying the law; rather, I become righteous through faith in Christ. For God's way of making us right with himself depends on faith. I want to know Christ and experience the mighty power that raised him from the dead. I want to suffer with him, sharing in his death, so that one way or another I will experience the resurrection from the dead! (Philippians 3:8–11 NLT)

Now that's when I get uncomfortable and begin to squirm; I don't like the thought of suffering. It makes me unsettled to think I might look or sound strange to others. They may reject me or not want me around any longer. What will they think if we are really going into the world, announcing as Jesus told us to say that "the Kingdom of Heaven is near," praying and seeing sick people healed, the dead raised, and demons cast out? The religious organization of His day began to say Jesus was from Satan. What might they say of me?

That is the evidence I see of the cost Jesus paid. Love required great things of Him, and yet brought such great glory to God. Here is where many, including myself, at times, sit, wavering on the fence (not leaving the pews), unable to move. Yet there exists a dubious unrest in souls wanting, longing for more.

In this light, we become outcasts to the world while encountering the love of God. The irony is that somehow this makes us more complete and satisfied in our inner man. The Kingdom of God works this way: It takes what is and transforms it, making what is impossible possible, giving life where there was death. In the Kingdom, what doesn't exist comes into being with one word of God. Power to do what we have not the strength to do is made available as God's love fills us. It grows as I enter into greater intimacy with God. As I know Him and trust He knows me, my confidence in that love creates a strong foundation of trust that allows me to walk in obedience to His will.

It is from this foundation, as disciples then, that through that love we feed the hungry, clothe the needy, take care of the widows, forgive those that hurt us, start ministries, support missionaries, minister/pray for others, love the unlovely, comfort the brokenhearted, give hope to the hopeless, and even tithe. Not because it is easy or "normal," but because it is what God's love propels us to do. We are gifted to become the hands and feet of Jesus to a hurting and dying world. In the freedom of His love there are no confines requiring us to fit in to what is seen as service within the church (greeting, working in the nursery, etc.), although these services are certainly not bad or unimportant. Unlimited opportunity and divine appointments await us in the abundance of His amazing love. We are simply to walking in obedience to whatever His voice is calling us to do every moment of our lives, trusting that He will provide everything we need.

This love flowing through the body of Christ will reveal primarily two things. First, that we the Church belong to Christ and are His disciples. This is evidenced by how we love each other.

"So now I am giving you a new commandment: Love each other. Just as I have loved you, you should love each other. Your love for one another will prove to the world that you are my disciples." (John 13:34–35 NLT)

Second, that this same love is available for everyone, it is to be demonstrated by us having compassion and meeting their needs. John describes this in his epistles, saying:

If someone has enough money to live well and sees a brother or sister in need but shows no compassion—how can God's love be in that person? Dear children, let's not merely say that we love each other; let us show the truth by our actions. Our actions will show that we belong to the truth, so we will be confident when we stand before God. (1 John 3:17–19 NLT)

As the Church (people in the body of Christ) loves one other, it demonstrates to others that we belong to Christ and that our lives have been changed by Him. Unconditional love is not a commodity that the world possesses, only those who have experienced this love from their heavenly Father have the capacity to love in such a way. Not because of who they are, but because of what God has done in them.

Unconditional love was a foreign land to me as well; for so many years I had not experienced it in my home or relationships. Even though I had been a "Christian" for most of my life, I had not encountered such a force until God interrupted my life with a wakeup call out of the darkness.

It was during the time I was separated from my husband because of the undealt-with pain of the past. I was running from anyone and everyone who truly cared for me. My own shame and self-hate drove me to a place of emotional breakdown. I was making choices that led me deeper down the dark path of my own depression.

One day a friend and I went to a Kansas City Chief's football game. We spent the afternoon drinking and celebrating. As we drove out of the parking lot, my friend, who was driving, ran into a boy walking to his car. Fear overcame me as the police quickly arrived and took her away. I was instructed that I could take the car; however, I was fully aware *I* was in no condition to drive. If you can remember the time (I'm truly dating myself) before cell phones, then you understand I had nowhere to go and no way to get ahold of anyone. I was escorted to the administrative headquarters to use their phone.

One after another I called people to come get me and found everyone busy or they didn't care. Finally, I got ahold of my boss who was attending a family function and he said he would come after it was over. Because the stadium was closing, I had to wait outside. Sitting on the curb, I watched all the players, owners, and finally the workers leave. As I lifted my head and looked around, I saw that I was totally alone, everyone had left. A deep sense of where my life was began to dawn on me as I saw how I had pushed God, my family, husband and true friends away.

Later that evening, after arriving home, I fell into my bed and began to sob; wells of grief, sorrow and pain flowed out. Through my sobs I heard myself whisper over and over again, "O God…O God…O God." When I woke the next morning, I knew deep within myself that God was asking me to call Mike, my husband. I battled what seemed to be the craziest thoughts for several hours, until I picked up the phone to make the call. It had been six months since I had talked to him. When he answered, I relayed the story of what had happened at the game the evening before. It was in the next moment that God used my husband's words to break through all the hardness of my heart to reveal His unconditional love to me. Mike's response was, "I'll be right there." More than that, I knew God was saying the same thing to me. After all I had done, and as underserving as any kindness was, I received through those words God's true acceptance for the first time. *God was taking me out the smallness of my own understanding into the greatness of who He really is!*

It has been a long journey with Jesus since that time, into a place of wholeness and completeness. After years I now know and have experienced the trustworthy and unconditional love of God to where my soul can now say, "I am God's and He is mine." With each step toward Him, He encourages me into greater obedience to what He has for me. Loving others and sharing what His love has done for me is the great joy of my life. God has used many beautiful people within the Church throughout this journey to walk along side of me and encourage me into deep intimacy with Him. Together we are learning as true disciples of Christ that we must take steps forward, out of the confines that have been normal, "doing church," into the adventure of "being the church." This is living outside the box, no longer "playing church" or holding to the expectations of others. Freely loving God and others—becoming the Church—being like Jesus to the world! I'm truly out of the *game*!

"Go and announce to them that the Kingdom of Heaven is near. Heal the sick, raise the dead, cure those with leprosy, and cast out demons. Give as freely as you have received!" (Matthew 10:7–8 NLT)

Jesus came and told his disciples, "I have been given all authority in Heaven and on earth. Therefore, go and make disciples of all the nations, baptizing them in the name of the Father and the Son and the Holy Spirit. Teach these new disciples to obey all the commands I have given you. And be sure of this: I am with you always, even to the end of the age." (Matthew 28:18–20 NLT)

95267298R00055

Made in the USA
Lexington, KY
06 August 2018